A CHRISTIAN APPROACH T

FROM STRESS

TO

STRENGTH

BY

JOHN BANKS

MOORLEY'S Print & Publishing

© Copyright 1997

All rights reserved. No part of this publication may be
reproduced, stored in a retrieval system, or
transmitted, in any form or by any means,
electronic, mechanical, photocopying, recording
or otherwise, without the prior
written permission of the publishers.

British Library Cataloguing in Publication Data.
A catalogue record for this book is available
from the British Library.

MOORLEY'S Print & Publishing
23 Park Rd., Ilkeston, Derbys DE7 5DA
Tel/Fax: (0115) 932 0643

ISBN 0 86071 500 0

CONTENTS

    page

Foreword by Bishop Roy Williamson   iv

Introduction   v

Chapter 1	IT COULD HAPPEN TO YOU	1
Chapter 2	IT HAPPENED TO ME	4
Chapter 3	OBSESSIONAL FEARS	8
Chapter 4	FAITH AND FEAR	11
Chapter 5	MEDICINE AND PRAYER	15
Chapter 6	SPIRITUAL GROWTH	21
Chapter 7	MEDICATION HELP	28
Chapter 8	PSYCHOLOGICAL HELP - BEHAVIOUR THERAPY	31
Chapter 9	THE WOUNDED HELPER	33
Notes		37

FOREWORD

Here is a book that needed to be written, a human story that needed to be told. It is the personal account of a journey from light through darkness into light. Within all the pressures of modern living many find themselves driven to make a similar journey. Here is a sensitive reflection that cannot fail to bring hope to others who have passed or are passing that way.

The author is a most able and gifted pastor. Over the years he has engaged in an effective ministry of healing and I have been one among many who have been moved by his reflections on 'Christ, the wounded Healer'. Now he writes out of the experience of his own wounds.

How many of us have stood alongside friends who may be suffering from some form of depression and said, "I understand. I know exactly how you are feeling." Yet, deep down, we know there is a superficiality about our words because, if we are honest, we really have no idea at all how the depressed person is feeling. We can theorize. We can draw lessons from the scriptures. We can give examples of other people who have passed that way. But, so often, our words lack conviction.

John Banks's words carry both conviction and authenticity because they have been hammered out on the anvil of personal suffering. His experience, bitter though it was at times, was carried into the larger context of Cross and Resurrection. Thus a painful journey became a pilgrimage that moved through darkness to light, from despair to hope.

This superb little book will increase our understanding of and empathy towards those who suffer from mental illness and, if we will allow, it will lead us towards a greater wholeness.

+Roy Williamson
Bishop of Southwark

INTRODUCTION

Many suffer in secret from intense fears and anxieties. For some considerable time I suffered secretly. Had I been aware earlier of the medical and spiritual implications of my problem I would have found appropriate help and been spared much suffering. It would have been of great assistance also to have known of someone with a similar problem who had been helped to tackle it.

This book is written in the hope that it might reach some of those who suffer secretly - indeed any afflicted with the torment of fear, and give light in their darkness.

Indeed it is written for all who grapple with the fact of suffering not only in their own lives but also in the lives of others, and especially some of the most intractable of all suffering, namely mental suffering. This is an area where a big educational task remains to be done with the help not just of doctors but also of patients who have actually experienced these mental traumas. This is a book written from the heart in a very frank way by an ordinary Christian who has had to battle with such anguish and who has come through to a deeper perspective on life and faith and the nature of suffering. I trust as such it will be a help to very many.

The stressful age in which we live has served to aggravate mental health problems and about one in six of the population need psychiatric help.

There is still much stigma to overcome and many misunderstandings. These are high-lighted by the stupid remark levelled at so many sufferers, "pull yourself together." This reveals tragic ignorance of the medical and spiritual implications of mental illness. Even caring people including many Christians are guilty of such mistaken views. This is pastorally damaging and just adds to the patient's sense of helplessness and guilt. This book is written to help to rectify these matters and to offer a positive Christian approach that gives hope, and affirms sufferers in the love of God, itself a great therapy.

I find many people who are troubled by bad thoughts that intrude in an unwanted way. These formed the core of some of my severest fears and anxieties, particularly the dread that I might inadvertently say them. I didn't realise for a long time that these were the basis of a condition known as obsessional neurosis. They preoccupied my mind and in time seriously disrupted my whole life-style.

These intense fears were very distressing emphasising the loss of control, which is a feature of much mental illness. They were accompanied by compelling urges to check that I hadn't caused any harm. There is a bit of the checking personality in many people. At its very basic level it is to be seen in the person who has to go back and check they've locked the front door, or in the person who keeps checking that electrical appliances are safely switched off. Significantly there are many in caring work whose personalities are particularly prone to this sort of difficulty.

This book will doubtless ring a bell with many people who have deep-seated fears, those who are of a perfectionist nature, anxious to get things right, and with a general desire to please. Such people often find it hard to express anger and this can aggravate their problem.

"From Stress to Strength" shows that there is a way through these ordeals with help and that many positives can emerge out of the negatives.

Some when tackling mental health problems think the approach should be solely medical, others that it should be solely spiritual. My contention born of much experience, is that it should be both medical and spiritual, as God is working through both. That is the main theme of my book.

I am grateful to the Consultant Psychiatrist, Dr. Richard Turner, who looked after me during my illness. He has kindly read the draft of the book and made helpful suggestions. I am grateful also to Dr. N. Macaskill, Consultant Psychotherapist, and to Mr. Brian Spencer, Librarian of Mapperley Hospital for pointing me to helpful medical sources of information, and to Sue, my wife, for typing the manuscript and for making helpful comments in her customary discerning way.

Finally, I thank Bishop Roy Williamson for his pastoral and spiritual care of me during my mental anguish and for so willingly writing a foreword to this book.

To Sue, for her part

in the victory over the

fears and much else

CHAPTER 1
IT COULD HAPPEN TO YOU

Most people pay more attention to physical health than to mental health. Indeed many skate round mental health issues if they can possibly do so. Usually those with physical illness get much more sympathy than those in mental suffering. Yet much mental illness can be more traumatic than physical affliction. This is often the feeling of those who have suffered both. A powerful example of this came in the comments of Lady Tebbit in a Radio 4 'Desert Island Discs' programme. She was severely paralysed in the bomb outrage at Brighton's Grand Hotel. For years she had also suffered mental illness as a result of post-natal depression. When asked if she could make the difficult choice as to which illness she would rather cope with, she replied without hesitation that it would be the paralysis.

Sad to say many stigmatize those with mental illness. Some just feel out of their depth and this is true of many Christian clergy and congregations. Some are just embarrassed by it. This was clear from the 'Panorama' broadcast of the Princess of Wales when she spoke of reactions to her post-natal depression and subsequent bulimia. Yet the fact is that one in six of the population seek psychiatric help at some stage in their lives. An increasing number suffer from mental stress, and most people have an aspect of a mental hang-up in their character.

For example think of those of us with various phobias, perhaps of spiders or mice or blood or death. Paul Tournier, a distinguished doctor, with long experience, said that the most tenacious fear that he met with in his patients was fear of death. This is confirmed in my own wide experience in pastoral work. Sometimes the fear is more of the process of dying than of death itself. All this is mirrored in the attitudes towards bereavement.

Often it causes embarrassment and the bereaved can find themselves virtually isolated in their grief. Many become mentally ill through unresolved grief. In this fast moving age many are not given time to work through their grief. They are expected to get over it as if they were dealing with a dose of 'flu'.

Think of those who always need to have an escape route and sit near the door in a crowded room, a touch of claustrophobia. Think of those who are happy at home but anxious about going out - a touch of agrophobia there. Grace Sheppard, the Bishop of Liverpool's wife, was afflicted in this way and describes her experiences movingly in a book entitled "An Aspect of Fear". As she says the root worry is fear of losing control, of not being able to handle what might happen. Such worry is at the core of much mental illness. It is encouraging to many sufferers when prominent people like this write publicly of their mental health difficulties. It gives people hope.

Or again think of those people who have a chip on their shoulders, who feel the world is against them and are suspicious of people's intentions - a touch of paranoia there.

Think of the many women who suffer a period of distressing depression after the birth of their baby. In some cases they are tormented by an urge to hurt their baby, rather than to bring loving help. This is so contrary to their real self's wishes but it shows what distorted thoughts can plague the mind - the very opposite of what we really want. This is a condition which is nowadays usually readily responsive to medical treatment. In the old days the patients were often put into a mental hospital for life.

Think of those of a perfectionist nature who constantly have to check things are right. They are tormented by bad thoughts and often perform rituals of hand-washing etc. Sometimes their fear is of electrical appliances in case they might not see to them properly and so cause damage. There is something of obsessional neurosis in all this. Think of those who are depressed through redundancy or a relationship problem or stress at work.

Think of those who are hyper-active with grandiose ideas - alternating with depression. When they're on a 'high' they can have an exaggerated sense of their own importance, be extravagant with money and have delusions of grandeur. Such mood swings are symptomatic of manic depression.

Think of those who are much given to drawing attention to themselves and are often very manipulative - a touch of the hysterical personality there.

Think of those with low self-esteem who feel they can only be acceptable if they have a very slim figure and nearly starve themselves to achieve this - something of anorexia there.

The reason for embarrassment about people with mental illness is therefore that it is too close for comfort. It reminds us of the hang-ups in our own nature. We are reluctant to come to terms with them or even to acknowledge them.

As with many of life's hazards people tend to think "it could never happen to me". However, it can and often does. Even mature Christians are not immune. An increasing number of people are seeking help for mental health problems.

Some Christians think that they should be immune. They feel an inner sense of shame. They feel that they are defective in faith if such problems afflict them. Many suffer in secret because of this instead of getting necessary help, both medical and spiritual. This problem is compounded when in Churches or Christian fellowship groups that very attitude of alleged defect in faith is taken towards them. I have met many patients who have felt a sense of rejection and unworthiness because of this.

Often this judgmental attitude is accompanied by an ignorance of the nature of mental illness. Along with this goes a distrust of the medical approaches. People are wrongly told to throw away their tablets, and are subjected to a misguided spiritual ministry which aims at 'getting the devil' out of the patient. This leaves the sufferer in an even worse state. They wrongly feel themselves to be evil. Their low self-esteem is made worse. They need the partnership of understanding pastoral ministry with prayer *and* medicine. God is working through *both*.

Many things can trigger a mental illness, the roots of which often go back right to infancy and childhood. For example it may be a sudden shock or an accident. It may be through loss or worry. It may be the result of chemical changes brought about in a mother through childbirth, or the pressures of growing up or examinations. It may be through the trauma of sexual abuse, or a depressing environment.

These sort of factors can affect the chemistry of our mind and so our thought patterns as well as our emotional states.

It comes as a relief to many to know these things, and to be aware of the help that is available.

There is still much educational work about mental health to be done with the general public, including schools.

Yes, it could happen to you. It happened to me and has done to countless others. However take heart, God can bring positives out of our negatives if we seek the necessary help.

CHAPTER 2
IT HAPPENED TO ME

It was dusk in 1962 as I was driving in the outskirts of Oxford doing some pastoral visiting from the city centre Church of St. Aldate's where I was based. At a road junction on an estate there was a sudden bump. I had collided with a moped rider who came off his machine. I stopped and made sure he wasn't injured. He said that an arm hurt, but he was able to continue his journey. There was no damage to either vehicle. Stupidly I never asked him for his name and address. That omission was to be of great cost to my peace of mind.

Fears, that I came to understand later were obsessional, began to intrude into my thoughts. I felt I must check to see if he was all right. This was to be but the prelude to excessive checking about a whole range of things usually based on the syndrome of fear that I might be hurting someone rather than helping them. You can imagine the torment that this brought to a person like myself, a priest, and so expected to be a carer. Indeed any of a caring nature are distressed by such thoughts. The fear of living a denial of all that I stood for, and of damaging others, began to haunt me.

The immediate torment was the fear brought on by the remorse and guilt over the accident - fear that I might have caused the moped rider more serious injuries than was realised at the time.

I checked at several local doctors' surgeries to see if anyone with an arm injury had presented themselves. It was all to no avail. I might have *really* hurt someone and I couldn't even find him to apologise!

I tried to recall his moped's registration number but that eluded me. I hazarded a guess at it and asked a friend in the police to check it out for me - it turned out to be a corporation dust-cart at Windsor!

Gradually I had to come to terms with the fact that I would never succeed in my quest to check that all was well with the moped rider. Moreover a pattern of fear and checking had started in my life that became more and more entrenched. Driving was to prove a particular burden. My imagination began to run away with me - what tricks it played! I kept imagining I was the cause of an accident - shades of the moped rider! The problem was compounded in that I found myself doubting my own powers of judgment. On two or three occasions I even went to the police to tell them I might have caused an accident.

As I drove along I might think, 'Was that just a bump in the road or a bump because I'd knocked someone over?' 'Did I see someone loom up in front of my car or was it my imagination?' I would look through my rear driving mirror and think 'Was that a body that I'd hit lying prostrate in the road or just a dark shadow?'

I had a driving refresher course from an ex-police instructor to try to regain my confidence, but the problem remained. It was an ordeal to go out in the car. In my imagination I felt I might have perpetrated a lot of hurt. I would stop the car or retrace my ground to check if all was well. Worry about it might well continue into the next day. Checking never brought real satisfaction - it usually led to more checking.

Gradually the urge to check was becoming more and more compulsive, and if I didn't check I became tense and anxious. This was long before I had ever heard of a mental illness condition called obsessional neurosis which afflicts a large number of people, many of whom suffer in secret. "An obsessive-compulsive may keep his experience secret for years and somehow struggle to manage an apparently normal life."[1]

The obsessive fears that beset me didn't just concern the car. They began to creep into virtually everything. On the work front I would be checking again and again that I'd got marriage registers correct in case I hadn't properly married people! I can remember going to a football dressing room to check a bridegroom's marriage certificate - he'd gone straight from his wedding to play in a football match! This inability to trust one's own judgment is devastating.

I would be walking along a pavement and feel I might have trodden on a baby, anxiously looking back to check all was well. Passing a person as I walked along I would fear that I'd pushed them into the road, and caused them to be hurt. Again I felt the urge to look back and check. I would put my hands in my pockets as an antidote to this, so that they could be up to no wrong. As a worker in the sphere of mental health much later, I recall talking with a patient whose obsession about knives caused him to do the same thing. He then could be sure he hadn't plunged a knife into someone.

A feature of checking can be in relation to switches, checking they are safely in the correct position. I found this took a colossal amount of time and effort, often checking not just three times, but nine times and more.

I thought that I was contaminating the water coming out of the taps by accidentally touching them with germ-infested hands. So I washed the taps as well as my hands over and over again. I was fighting exhausting battles with invisible germs. You can imagine the problems that going to the toilet presented. Washing or taking a shower was a big ordeal. Sometimes in a patient's behaviour such excessive washing can be interpreted as a symbolic cleansing of impulses and memories.

It was a big problem to turn off a tap. I checked again and again that it was turned off properly. My worry was that water would escape and flood the building. Again underneath was the fear of damaging people.

The same applied to switches. They were obsessively checked in case I had unwittingly caused an electrical fault and so put people at risk. Simply to turn off a switch was an ordeal which caused enormous anxiety. A terrible dread would pass through my mind that I might inadvertently kill someone.

At times I would sense how absurd some of the obsessive thoughts and checkings were, but I seemed at the mercy of them and unable to overcome the compulsive urges that came. The mental anguish was enormous. The sheer volume and intensity of the thoughts overwhelmed me. Even more distressing were the bad thoughts that I had about people which I was terrified I might speak or write. All this mental torment made me feel very depressed.

I was never suicidal but often I just wanted to die, to go to sleep and not wake up again. I felt I was being destroyed as a person. From being a happy out-going man I had become a fearful wreck. I felt I'd had enough. There seemed to be no point in living - such was the mental darkness. I thought of our Lord's cry of dereliction from the Cross, "My God, my God why have you forsaken me?"[2] Later I was to come to appreciate more the words of Bishop F.R. Barry, "Nothing less than the Cross and the cry of dereliction can begin to awaken some trust in God and reconciliation with life - an atonement with meaning in existence."[3]

Sleep itself was very difficult. It is ironic that when we are mentally exhausted and so in need of sleep it can so easily elude us. Our minds are so wound up that we find it hard to switch off. Indeed my mind felt like a record player stuck in a groove. I was very conscious of the pressure and tension feelings in my head and face.

Much of the fears seem ludicrous now but at the time they were all too real. It was hard to trust my judgment that all was really well. I began asking Sue, my wife, and others if they would check for me, but even that didn't satisfy. I couldn't even trust them and I could see that this naturally became irritating to them. I have learnt that a form of obsessive thinking is persistent doubting.

A patient may feel unsure whether or not he has behaved wrongly, or may have to look several times to see if he has turned off the gas. "For example, a woman who had impulses to strike children in prams, would when a pram had passed her wonder if she had in fact hit or killed the child. She would then become intensely and painfully preoccupied with trying to reconstruct in her mind exactly what had happened, becoming in the process more and more certain that she had killed the child, requiring repeated reassurance that she had not, but never quite reaching certainty either way, always doubting[4]."

I was thinking bad thoughts that a person might be a cheat or an adulterer, and feeling guilty. Then I would fear that I had actually said that thought and so maligned their good character.

It's not hard to imagine the shame and the distress that this caused. Just to have the thoughts was bad enough. Again I might be damaging people instead of helping them, this time by impugning their good name.

So normal conversation that I had previously enjoyed began to be clouded with intense fears, mounting to panic - and my sense of humour was sadly diminishing. I find it hard to convey the mental pain of all this as it gradually began to dominate my life - the dread, the panic that would surge over me.

I would desperately try a balancing statement to try and rectify the situation, especially any possible leaking of the thoughts into words. If I'd had a bad thought about someone I would say something good about them, even if it meant introducing their name into the conversation in order to do so - often this would seem very contrived.

The bad thoughts would come in Services too, something many Christians experience, and I was afraid I might be saying them - shocking thoughts in a sacred service - what torment! I have learnt recently that John Bunyan suffered from similar torment. Later the Consultant Psychiatrist was to assure me that I would never actually say these thoughts or write them - explaining that patients like myself never did - but still I couldn't be convinced. I thought one or two might slip through the net - that I might be the exception to the rule.

To have bad thoughts does not mean that we ourselves are bad - it is part of the flawed human condition. This cognitive therapy, the realistic way we look at life is an important part of the healing process.

Even conversation at home with my family was subject to the same fears caused by the intrusive thoughts - there was little let-up. Mental illness often puts a big strain on marriage and family life, as it did in my own case. The resentment is not so much with the patient as with the illness that makes the sufferer unable to fulfil their normal role, and in some cases changes their personality. It would help if more patients realised this important distinction. Sometimes patients are so bogged down with their mental health problem as to be unaware of its devastating effect on their family. It helps if the doctor does consult with close family and so bring them into the picture more and into the treatment.

It is particularly distressing that the negative thoughts were often bad unwanted thoughts. I have known clean-living people be obsessed with crude thoughts. It seems ironic that it is frequently good-living people who are afflicted in this way. We need medical as well as spiritual help in combating them. This powerful combination in time brought me to a good recovery and a deeper appreciation of life and the Christian interpretation of it.

CHAPTER 3
OBSESSIONAL FEARS

Obsessions show themselves as recurring thoughts or ideas which are frightening or distressing. Usually they are accompanied by rituals which are called compulsive because you cannot stop yourself performing them. For example, someone with an obsession about safety might believe they have left electrical appliances in an unsafe state. They feel forced to check again and again that everything is correctly switched off. Someone with an obsession about cleanliness may believe that their hands are contaminated with dirt or germs. This distressing thought will compel them to wash their hands needlessly over and over again throughout the day.

The purpose behind the various rituals is an attempt to give protection against the consequences of a potential danger. The rituals may give some relief, but then the anxiety starts up again. The urge to perform the rituals returns. All this of course becomes very time consuming. It gradually seriously disrupts normal daily routine.

Thoughts that are senseless can recur, coming out of the blue. Some sufferers repeat over and over again certain magical acts based on numbers. For some patients the thoughts are highly charged ideas, for example that they might have killed someone. The rituals are developed as an attempt to neutralize the danger and reduce the level of anxiety. The basic thought is that if I don't perform this ritual someone might get hurt.

I would sometimes aim at three checks so that the checking would be aligned to the theme of the Trinity. Often this would develop into multiples of three. One sufferer I've met did his rituals round the number four and that had religious significance also.

A distinguished psychiatrist Aubrey Lewis, explains obsessional fears in this way. The patient complains of a mental experience in which there is a feeling of subjective compulsion. He doesn't want that feeling and in fact does his utmost to get rid of it.

Dr. David Enoch, a Consultant Psychiatrist at Liverpool, points out that common amongst intrusive thoughts are "harming loved ones and obsessions about dirt and death."[5] He tells us that the sufferers cannot pull themselves out of these feelings which cause much distress. The thoughts restrict personal activity. They cause difficulty in doing work, and preserving relationships with others. He states that most professional people such as clergy and doctors have obsessional traits.

It has been pointed out that the "three essential elements are the feeling of subjective compulsion, the resistance to it, and the retention of insight."[6] Phobias are defined as intense fears of things which would not be a problem for the average person.

Most people have some obsessional traits in their mind and behaviour. It could be the urge to check that they've locked the door or seen to the safety of the electrical appliances in the house. It could be that the urge for order compels them to straighten and line up pictures that hang on the wall. Our play activities when we were children perhaps showed some obsessional characteristics. Perhaps we avoided cracks in the paving stones or touched every lamp post in the street. Some patients might feel that if they don't touch various objects something tragic will befall them or the people they love.

It has been noted that the obsessive patient is often an agile-thinking and reliable person who finds it difficult to express anger. That combined with a perfectionist nature and a strong desire to please is a kind of seed-bed for the growth of obsessional fears. Certainly I recall from my own childhood a strong influence towards rectitude and a desire to please. As with phobias, a traumatic event can also be the triggering cause of obsessive thoughts or behaviour, as can heredity or early environment.

About one tenth of all people suffer bits of this illness in the course of a life-time but only a minority seek treatment. Some delay seeking help because they might be thought to be mad, but it rarely develops into severe mental illness. The sooner we seek help the better.

Many suffer secretly. A patient was a school-teacher for many years. She went through constant checking rituals without her colleagues ever being aware of it. She would stay on at work after hours to go through these checks until she was exhausted. If, for example, it was prior to a parents' evening, she would check her pupils' books for ages to ensure she had marked them correctly, so that all would be in order when they went on view. Another patient was a G.P. He found that he was continually checking prescriptions he'd written out. You can imagine the traumas this caused him. He was terrified he might damage a patient through prescribing the wrong dosage.

There have been some helpful programmes on television and constructive articles in some of the press recently dealing with mental health issues. These have included examples of those who struggle with obsessional fears and rituals. This helps the education of the general public. It also can enable sufferers to see that they are not alone in their struggles. Hopefully it will encourage more people to seek help if they are not already doing so.

There was for instance a helpful article in the "Observer" newspaper magazine in March 1990 on 'Obsessive Compulsive Disorder'. As it pointed out, "A few individual cases of obsessive compulsive disorder have been reported in the medical literature over the past 150 years, but only recently have we learnt of the large number of adolescents and adults who suffer with it - and suffer secretly."[7]

The article, by Dr. Judith Rapoport, points out that all of the problems of sufferers have common themes. "Those afflicted with the disorder can't trust their ordinary good judgment, can't trust their eyes that see no dirt, or really believe that the door is locked. Patients know they have done nothing harmful but in spite of this good sense they go on checking."

She gives an example of a sufferer who might wash her hands 30-40 times in one day, wash and re-wash the lavatory, and wash her hair anything up to ten times.

A young man in his early twenties was obsessional about knives, and he too was seeking to grow spiritually. He had a terrible struggle with the unwanted intrusive thoughts. However, with the combined help of medication and behavioural therapy techniques, and prayer, he eventually got a real measure of control over his obsessions and compulsions.

There was much with which I could identify. He had bad thoughts about hurting people, especially his mother. That naturally made him particularly distressed. He put his hands in his pockets to prevent them doing wrong when he was stricken with a bad thought. If he was in the kitchen with his mother, and there was a knife visible he would see himself plunging the knife into her. It was a terrible torment to him especially as he had a good relationship with her. She was very patient and understanding and did a lot to help him. He would seek reassurance over his bad thoughts and checkings. Likewise his mother and the rest of the family knew that to comply with that would only give the obsessions a false credence in his eyes and so serve to reinforce them.

He worked very hard at the techniques of dismissing the thoughts, keeping a daily record of progress. I was able to share with him some of the methods that I had found helpful, and encouraged him to persevere. There were some set-backs. However, gradually he got a measure of control that enabled him to be discharged from hospital and resume normal life. He also became stronger in his Christian faith.

Another patient, this time an elderly lady, has obsessional fears stemming from an accident whilst travelling in a coach. She worries mainly about electrical appliances and gas fires and the safety of these things. She has a chart on her kitchen wall listing the various gadgets and puts a tick against them when they have been checked. Last thing at night is a particularly tormenting time for her. Even when her husband has gone round to see that everything is all right, she will feel compelling urges to get out of bed and go downstairs and check appliances.

I have told her of the various behavioural therapy techniques to try and help her. She also finds great strength in the ministry of laying on of hands with prayer.

There is a way through these sufferings with the help of medication, behavioural therapy, and prayer. These can reduce the anxiety which is such a driving force to the obsessions. It reduces their intensity and frequency.

CHAPTER 4
FAITH AND FEAR

What was the place of faith in all this? I came to the view that fear is a much greater challenge to faith than doubt - doubts can be real growing points but these crippling fears were so negative and destructive.

After my recovery I read a passage in Stuart Blanch's book "Living by Faith" where he shows that the contrast is drawn in the Bible very strongly between faith and fear, when we might have expected the contrast to be between faith and unbelief (e.g. Mark 4 v.35 to 5 v.43). He speaks frankly of the tensions caused by fear in his own life. He writes of living uncomfortably near the edge of his own endurance. Indeed he toppled over it once or twice. He asked his doctor the cause of tension and got the reply, "There is only one cause of tension and that is fear." He goes on to say that "it is precisely because it is so difficult to identify the cause of fear that it is so potent."[8] He speaks of the signs of God's presence even in the midst of the most intransigent and fearful circumstances, and that we cannot drift outside God's love and care. The assurance of His love is the greatest answer to our fears.

Yes, something of that did get through to me but it is hard to grasp it when your mind is so tormented.

I related to so much in the Psalms about being in a pit and feeling trapped in my own thoughts. "Fear and trembling have beset me: horror has overwhelmed me. I said, Oh, that I had the wings of a dove! I would fly away and be at rest."[9] "They spread a net for my feet - I was bowed down in distress."[10] "How long must I wrestle with my thoughts and everyday have sorrow in my heart?"[11]

When I was in Mapperley Hospital[12] for treatment for my condition I derived comfort from many of the Psalms. They express in such a frank way our own inner conflicts.

I never doubted the reality of God during my long illness although often He seemed distant - but it all seemed so unfair and meaningless. Later it was to dawn on me more that so much of life is unfair. I realised that Jesus on the Cross plumbed the depths of this also so that we might not feel that God has left us at the mercy of life's injustices. Indeed He is sharing in these things with us. I read recently that we need to remember that when God seems far away He hasn't moved.

I didn't believe that God had sent the illness to me but it was very difficult to see why He'd allowed it to happen. I don't believe that God does send illness to people and have never been able to relate to the view that crosses of suffering are laid upon us by Him. "It's my cross," you hear some people say in a resigned way. I do believe that suffering can produce responses that can be redemptive and that we can learn important lessons and qualities through it. I believe that God working through us, can over-ride and transform our sufferings for His own purposes. He does so in a creative way which we cannot always see at the time - but that is a different matter.

We have to face the fact that some people grow through suffering while others become bitter or despairing. Why is this? Surely it is the quality of the help, prayer and love that surround us that is crucial, plus the way we respond to these things. The faith factor in this is obvious. It is not the suffering itself which matures people but the way we react to it.

The Cross of Jesus is surely the proof that God doesn't send suffering to us but comes to share it with us. Dr. Sheila Cassidy who has been through much suffering herself, as well as caring for patients, in her book "Sharing the Darkness" speaks of "belief in a God who both permits suffering and is somehow deeply involved in his creation and his creatures, although we are at a loss to understand his ways."[13] God is in the pain is her conclusion. That surely is true of both physical and mental pain.

Some Gestapo guards were taunting a group of prisoners-of-war as they tortured a fellow prisoner. "Where is your God now?" they asked derisively. "He is there, He is there," shouted the prisoners pointing to the tortured man.

Since my boyhood I have been greatly influenced by the life and writings of F.R. Barry the Bishop of Southwell who ordained me. He was a great man of God, and in my sufferings his words gave me a lot of strength. He underwent a lot of personal suffering which clothes his words with even greater power. He has been described by Adrian Hastings as one of the sanest clerics of his time.

In an article in the "Times" newspaper Russell Barry wrote these words, "In a universe evolving and still unfinished in which there is suffering, wastage and disaster, the Creator's love suffers with his children; through that knowledge what can be barren and life-destroying may be redeemed into creative trust. Christian experience has affirmed that nothing, life or death, things present or things to come, can separate us from the love of God which is in Christ Jesus our Lord. I do not say that this is an 'answer', but it is a light which illuminates the mystery and shines unquenched in the hour of darkness."

He pointed out that life indeed seems "to be designed as to put a premium on courage"[14]. He saw that what matters most is not the things that happen to us but the faith and courage with which we meet them.

Some of his words came to mind in my hours of darkness and gave me hope. He wrote so frankly in his autobiography, 'Period of my Life'[15], of his own vulnerability and of how he needed the ministry and support of people. I felt so vulnerable myself. Vulnerability is not something people, especially in the caring agencies, are quick to admit, but it lies at the heart of our life. As Dr. Sheila Cassidy puts it in her book 'Good Friday People', "The great liberating truth is that we are all vulnerable wounded people and that is the way God made us. If this great insight seems a touch banal, forgive me, but like so many other self-evident truths, we don't actually live it!"[16] She speaks of learning during a period of psychotherapy that she was acceptable, even loveable, as a person and really very like other people.

My illness certainly taught me the truth of our vulnerability. We need to receive as well as to give. It is not weakness to admit this. It is strength, draws us closer to people, and makes us more able to help them. As mental health patients say to me now, "You understand us, John, you've been through it yourself."

So we can share more effectively in the broken-ness of people. There are so many hurt people out there. It's not easy to admit that we are vulnerable. We like to feel we are in control. We find it hard to admit our need for healing of these wounds and inadequacies, to God, to others, and to ourselves.

This is one of the main ways I was helped to grow during my lengthy illness. It has drawn me much closer to people. It has helped me to be less judgmental, more forgiving, more loving, more understanding, more prayerful, more ready to share.

All this shouldn't be a cause of surprise. After all we follow in the steps of a wounded Saviour.

Even though my sense of humour was diminished, at times I could raise a smile. Talking of F.R. Barry I would recall some of the many humorous anecdotes about him, as well as his profound writings on suffering. The legacy of his war wounds as a Chaplain in the 1914-18 War caused increasing deafness, but even that affliction had its lighter side. When someone shouted to him about three times, "Your car is at the door Bishop," he got the reply, "Put it on my desk will you?!" - a tall order!

His insights into suffering gave me hope. His last book was entitled 'To recover confidence.' In it he emphasises that we cannot just simply "read off a loving God from the world .... that faith was killed in action on the Somme and cremated at Auschwitz and Hiroshima - only this strange man with the Cross can give it to us, in his life and death and resurrection .... the divine compassion at the heart of things and a God to whom persons are dear."[17]

We need to remember that the Christian faith was born in tragedy. The symbol of Christ's victory is a Cross. Many sufferers find strength in this. I remember a young girl of eight with severe illness drawing a picture of the Crucifixion and underneath writing the word 'Victory'. You could see the victory of Jesus in her life, not bitter but positive, full of faith, prayer and love. It is this sort of experience which convinces us that love is stronger than fear, and life is stronger than death.

St. Paul, who also suffered much, gives expression to that in this great passage in his letter to Christians at Rome, "Neither life nor death, nor things present, nor things to come ..... can separate us from the love of God which is in Christ Jesus our Lord."[18] It is the quality of life opened up for us by Easter that makes it possible to say that.

When I was having treatment in hospital I can remember saying to myself, if I get better perhaps God will help me to be of some use to those struggling with mental darkness. Little did I dream that I would be doing Mental Health Chaplaincy work in the very same hospital a few years later. In fact many people who have been through mental suffering are a great help to others in the throes of it. That is one of the great values of mental health support groups, such as two I have helped with in Nottingham, the 'Four Seasons Group' and the 'Forest Group'. Such groups also help patients to integrate back into community life.

CHAPTER 5
MEDICINE AND PRAYER

The combined work of medicine and prayer, as personally experienced, has helped me greatly to work for that balance in people's understanding of health issues. It is so easy, as in all things, to polarize these. Some see them as rivals instead of partners. I very much believe in the wholeness model - namely that we are a trinity of body, mind and spirit - each inter-linking. Our ministry needs to be to the whole person in whatever discipline we work. We're not dealing with a piece of chemistry, a mind, or a soul, but with a person.

We shouldn't speak for example of the mentally ill, as if they were just cases. We shouldn't use hurtful terminology such as 'nut-cases', but speak of mentally ill people, or people with mental health problems. It was a wise French doctor who said, "there are no sicknesses only sick people." The term health or salvation is from a Hebrew root meaning "to be spacious". So it means freedom from all that cramps and confines. This is why that great pioneer surgeon Joseph Lister said that the two great requirements for those in medicine were "a warm and loving heart and truth in an earnest spirit" - love and truth, a powerful combination. In Jesus you never find one without the other.

This is why in the mission of the Church there should be no division between the personal Gospel and the social Gospel. Both need each other. People like General Booth of the Salvation Army saw this. He would speak of the need for "soup, soap and salvation." Archbishop Robert Runcie reminded us that our strategy should be the strategy of Jesus, "namely changing lives by love." We are not just concerned with the health of the individual but also with that of the community and creation as a whole. "Individuals and society cannot be fundamentally healed without a radical transformation. Religion is essential to this process. Personal renewal and renewal of society follow the same pattern. A return to God is a pre-condition for a return to health."[19]

As Morris Maddocks points out in his book 'Journey to Wholeness', "It is this concept of wholeness that holds out the greatest hope for the coming together of the healing professions."[20] The Church's involvement in the ministry of healing should emphasize this balance of medicine and prayer - that's why I prefer to call it the ministry of health and wholeness. Healing in the popular mind is so often reserved just for physical betterment. However we all know of people who can be wonderfully whole in their personalities, very much at peace with God and with life, whilst physically very sick. On the other hand there are others who are physically fit but inwardly very sick. An eminent modern doctor comments on the fact that whilst the ten lepers were all physically cured, the one who had also an inner transformation, the one who said 'thank you', was made whole. He writes, "some people are more at peace, more a whole personality with incurable disease than others are when sickness has been replaced by physical fitness."[21]

We need both medicine and prayer - God is working through both. In a graduation address to newly qualified medical students Joseph Lister said, "It is our proud office to tend the fleshly tabernacle of the immortal spirit." There's medicine in its true context. The medical and spiritual factors are complementary.

We need to remember also that prayer is not something we initiate, but something into which we enter. Part of its power rests in its corporate nature. There are times when all of us need to be carried in prayer. This is like the sick man in the Gospel narrative, being carried by four friends on a stretcher to Jesus.

Dr. Ruth Fowke writes of the power of prayer and other gifts of the Holy Spirit reaching areas in people inaccessible to secular therapies. She writes, "Many of these (secular therapies) can uncover past wounds, unravel complexes and accurately discern the inner plight of people but none known to me has the power to undo the past, to transform the tangled web woven deep in a person's history and remake an injured personality - in short to redeem the person. To pretend that they can is presumptuous, but to discard them because of their limitations is surely equally unreasonable."[22]

It is disturbing to find many people both in medicine and in the Churches who miss out on this balance. Some medics are tragically sceptical of the role of the spiritual factor: some Christians are sadly dismissive of the importance of the medical contribution.

A Christian's role is to help people arrive at a balanced authentic approach. The danger of belittling the medical aspect is put wittily in the limerick which runs:
"There was a faith healer of Deal
Who said 'although pain isn't real
When I sit on a pin
And it punctures my skin
I dislike what I fancy I feel!'"

One of the tragedies of the faith healing approach is that it deflects people from the authentic ministry. As Canon Douglas Webster points out, "Whatever type of healing a person may receive, it ultimately derives from one source only, namely from God, the source of life and energy. It is always God who heals. The doctor may treat, the priest may minister, the psychiatrist may analyse - but actual healing comes from God ...... The one title to be avoided at all costs is 'faith healing'. It is never faith as such that heals. Faith certainly enables us to receive healing, but it is always God who heals, not our faith."[23]

Guilt in patients is reinforced when some charismatic Christians ascribe mental illness to the activity of the devil. Some did when I was ill. The patients struggling with illness then have the needless added burden of anguish that they might in themselves be evil or possessed by evil. You can imagine the harmful effect on people who already think of themselves with very low self-esteem.

This hardly communicates the Gospel as one of love and acceptance, God affirming us as people. That is such a therapy especially with the mentally sick. I have discovered this more and more in mental health chaplaincy work.

Obviously some mental illness is caused by people being the victims of evil perpetrated on them (e.g. the patient you come across in later life whose low mental state has at root the hurt of being sexually abused as a child, perhaps by father or stepfather. The problem of sexual abuse is certainly not new. It was much more hushed up in the past). Some patients suffer because of the evil of being rejected in childhood by their parents. One lady told me that her parents had made it clear to her when she was a young child that she wasn't wanted because they really wanted a son instead of a daughter. She naturally had felt terribly rejected all her life.

Some people are made ill by exposing themselves to evil influences, e.g. the occult. The general public seem tragically unaware of the great harm that such experiences can bring. People mess about with tarot cards, ouija boards and other occult practices and many find themselves very disturbed mentally.

But in a vast number of illnesses there is no such link-up between sin and sickness. The ministry of Jesus clearly cut through such a general false equation (see St. John cp.9 verses 2-3). Jesus declares that a young man's blindness was not due to his own sin or that of his parents.

Some of the most lovely people suffer grievously. We all know of such people - wonderfully whole in their personalities. In them we see the triumph of the spirit. No lack of faith or prayer is responsible for their condition. Indeed they are powerful witnesses to the triumph of faith - witnesses to our suffering and risen Saviour. His touch has still its ancient power. The presence of the risen Christ with us and in us brings great inner strength.

Occasionally it seems as if recovery comes solely through spiritual means without medical agency or explanation. When this does happen it surely is not for the Church to chalk one up over medicine. Nor should medics be sceptical. All of us should just be thankful. Much more often God works through the partnership of both.

Illness can come to any of us - no one is immune. Naturally we ask "Why me?" - I certainly did in my anguish of suffering. However, I remember one day, as I sat in the hospital ward, coming to the realisation "Why not me?" Suffering is a fact of life - "Why should I be exempt?" Christians cannot claim some kind of immunity. Physical or mental sickness can come to anyone no matter how dedicated a Christian. We follow in the steps of a suffering Saviour. Nor do we have to be ill to suffer.

Anyone who is caring and sensitive to the needs of others suffers. And that should mean all of us. It is only some of the selfish and uncaring who appear 'to get away with it'. We should never envy them. It is what God helps us to do with it that is so important.

As Canon Michael Green puts it, "How people would rush to Christianity (and for all the wrong motives) if it carried with it an automatic exemption from sickness! What a nonsense it would make of Christian virtues like long-suffering, patience and endurance if instant wholeness were available for all the Christian sick! What a wrong impression it would give if salvation of physical wholeness were perfectly realised on earth whilst spiritual wholeness were partly reserved for heaven! What a very curious thing it would be if God were to decree death for all his children whilst not allowing illness for any of them."[24]

More thoughts about all this began to develop when I was in hospital. One or two extreme charismatic Christians were among the patients. They had an alienating effect by some of their attitudes, especially through the implication that our illnesses were caused by the work of the devil and could only really be dealt with spiritually. You could see the negative reaction of people on the ward. It just turned them off. It was hardly communicating the God of compassionate love "who in all their distress He too was distressed." (Isaiah 63 v.9). It was hardly communicating the truth that through the Cross God was sharing in all our adversity.

Much of God's compassionate love is channelled to us through people. The understanding of some of my fellow patients was particularly appreciated. Sue and I still keep contact with a few of them. I shall always remember with gratitude their companionship and friendship, the power of the fellowship of suffering, what Albert Schweitzer called "the fellowship of those who bear the mark of pain."

Some of them have since told me of the way in which they felt for me in the particular torments my illness brought me as a priest. Interestingly they were not all church people who had such sensitive compassion. This re-inforced my already held view of how much greater God's kingdom is than the limits of His Church. The Church for all its key role has no monopoly of God. It has been one of the contributions of liberal minded Christians to remind us of that truth.

He is at work in such a wide variety of ways. Would that all His agents would acknowledge the source of their insights! It seems to me that we are more likely to encourage such a response by affirming people in the love of God than by setting down demarcation lines between the Church and the world.

As J.B. Phillips puts it, "This country, at least, has many thousands of such 'unconscious Christians'. These men and women need to be told that what they are following, often spasmodically, is indeed ultimate reality and has been focused for us all in the recorded life of Jesus Christ. They already know something of love, but the garbled version of the Gospel which they hear from certain high-pressure evangelists does nothing to associate in their minds the ideas of love and of God."[25] Elsewhere he writes powerfully that people are basically loved into the Kingdom of God.

The setting of demarcation lines and the making of disparaging remarks about folk religion in my view don't help. My hospital experience, as much else, has revealed the unreality of many such demarcation lines.

Nothing is more powerful than the bonds created by shared suffering. God shares the darkness with us. As St. John says of Jesus, "The light shines in the darkness and the darkness has not overcome it."[26] And this again and again inspires the triumph of the Spirit, on the ways to the final and complete healing that awaits us in heaven, when we are given our spiritual resurrection body and where "God wipes away all tears from our eyes."

During my illness I came to realise to a greater extent than ever before the need for wholeness. Children can be very searching in their questions and comments. A boy asked his mother, "Mum, what is God doing all the time?" While Mum thought of an answer the boy said, "Is He mending broken things?" The boy was very near to the heart of the matter. Much of God's time is spent in mending broken people, and we all come within that description. We are all to a degree damaged people. However physically or mentally fit we may be, or however dedicated to God in spirit, we are none of us completely whole. In the lives of each one of us there are areas which need to come under the healing touch of God. We are none of us completely whole because in this earthly life we are none of us completely Christ's. It may be some ingrained prejudice, some fault which we have failed to overcome, some burden of guilt that remains on our conscience, some bitterness or resentment, some hurt that has deeply wounded us, perhaps stretching right back into early life, that we haven't handed over to God. Perhaps it is mental stress which robs us of inner peace, some relationship which is faulty, or perhaps a wound caused by bereavement, or perhaps some physical or mental condition or handicap which causes great frustration.

In so many ways we can feel broken in heart or in mind or body. We need that wholeness which God alone can bring, a wholeness above all in our personality and our relationships. That wholeness can come to those whose sickness finds no physical cure. As Canon George Bennett puts it, "The heart of healing is the heart of the Gospel: and the heart of the Gospel is the victory of Christ."[27]

Our church fellowships need to be less cluttered up with the organised system and more centred in the quality of the relationships which make for wholeness in Christ. This means small groups supplementing the life of the whole congregation. Where there is real accepting, forgiving love and prayerful care of one another, then God is clearly to be experienced. Such a therapeutic community, in the power of the Holy

Spirit, reaches out to others. The bad in human life is dealt with, the good is developed. It is not our achievement. It is the gift of the Holy Spirit. We need more such corporate experience. This is the great therapy of being affirmed in the love of God.

All this serves to emphasize the view that the main gap that the institutional Churches need to narrow is that between them and the very real spiritual feelings of many of the population. This, it seems to me, is the main challenge - not atheism, as Clifford Longley pointed out in an article about European Christianity in "The Times" a few years back. Only about five per cent of Europeans are atheists. If more church fellowships were to be loving, accepting and out-going in their caring work it would help. Many church people don't realise how off-putting much of the institutional life of the church can be to those struggling with particular pastoral needs. The system can so easily get in the way of the Saviour.

Hospital Chaplaincy work can often reach these people precisely because it is more personal and free of church institutional structures. In the hospital chaplaincy ministry we are thankfully free of many features of the system.

I found, during my recovery, that to spend hours each day visiting on hospital wards was a very revealing experience. It brought home to me the large part that spiritual factors play in health issues. Some time later I was to hear a hospital consultant make the very same point when he welcomed a new Chaplain at his Licensing Service.

This view is confirmed by a distinguished doctor, Sir James Watt. In his Presidential Address to the Institute of Religion and Medicine in October 1991, he points out that mechanistic systems of medicine may cure the disease or alleviate the symptoms, but often fail to heal the patient in the sense of giving them a meaning for life.

He states that "case histories from holistic medical practitioners, hospices and healing centres all suggest that modern medicine fails to take seriously enough the pre-clinical situation in which stress, violence, bereavement, suppressed emotions, guilt, grief, or a sense of isolation are to be found. We also need to know far more about the family and environmental background and how to elicit information."[28]

He believes that in the present more favourable climate, with growing emphasis on the way in which a patient is cared for by a multi-disciplinary team, the church has a golden opportunity. There is particular scope through counselling skills.

In this partnership prayer comes into its own and sick people in search of meaning to life can find wholeness.

CHAPTER 6
SPIRITUAL GROWTH

Many in illness learn a lot about patience, not an easily cultivated quality. Living in an age that craves for things on the instant makes it even harder. The healing of hurt minds usually takes quite a while.

I have been impressed with that wise statesman R.A Butler's autobiography, 'The Art of the Possible'. In it he quotes from a letter he'd written to Winston Churchill when Churchill had to retire from being Prime Minister through ill health. Butler, then Chancellor of The Exchequer, quoted some words of St. Teresa of Avila:
"Let nothing disturb thee,
Let nothing affright thee,
All passeth away.
God alone will stay
Patience obtaineth all things."[29]

However, it wasn't until I had to learn patience in the hospital situation and afterwards that I came to a real appreciation of this quality. Staff and patients certainly were for the most part very patient with me. Not only did I pester them for reassurance on the fears and checkings but also I got so distressed by the intrusive and unwanted thoughts that I would go round the ward saying "My mind is full of lies." Such was the volume of mental rubbish.

Some days seemed interminable. It was often hardest first thing in the morning when I would wonder how I could possibly get through another day. It was only very gradually that I came to appreciate more the importance of 'being' as well as 'doing'.

I must confess I found it hard to be patient with the nurses when they ignored my pleas for reassurance concerning my fears and checkings, especially as the urge to check was so strong and caused such panic and anguish. I felt that they were being hard-hearted in this regard but later I realised that they were right because checking just begets more checking and the intrusive thoughts and fears are reinforced. Checking is giving the mental rubbish credence.

Such a diverse community of people needed patience if you were to cope. A few of the patients were quite rough diamonds including one with an alcohol problem whom I met on a psychiatric ward in the University Hospital a few years later when I had started my Mental Health Chaplaincy work. Then he greeted me as a long-lost friend and informed others in the day-room that "I was in close touch with the main man up there," pointing heavenwards! A patient was sitting at a table in the corner of the room, dipping his biscuit in a cup of tea. He suddenly exclaimed, "I'm John the Baptist!" As quick as lightning the rough diamond said, "Well, I can see you're baptizing that biscuit all right!"

Enforced rest through illness gives you time to review your life. I had plenty of time to look back over my whole life, partly to see if there were any clues in my past history and family tree to account for my illness in addition to the road accident. I did realise that from being a small boy I had felt a strong pressure to please. Much greater perception into this came later. This built up an inner anger.

In an 'Observer' newspaper magazine article on Obsessive Compulsive Disorder, Dr. Peter Dally, a consultant psychiatrist, writes that "It is the confusion over how aggressive feelings can co-exist with those of love and security that is at the centre of obsessional states."[30]

I also looked at the nasty thoughts, and looked for features of my past life which might have contributed to them. I then brought them consciously into the forgiving, cleansing presence of God. Not only was this therapeutic in itself but I also resolved to avoid similar occasions for temptation and sin in the future.

By the grace of God I have managed to sustain this discipline with only occasional lapses. So again a cleansing process has been going on in my life. It needs vigilance and I am in no way complacent. It reminds me of the joke about a new Vicar coming to a parish and after a while a parishioner saying to him, "We never knew what sin was until you came, Vicar!"

I was spurred to concentrate on things that edify and cleanse the mind and its thought processes. I can appreciate even more the wisdom of St. Paul's words, "Whatever is true, whatever is noble, whatever is right, whatever is pure, whatever is lovely, whatever is admirable, think about such things."[31]

All this too has helped spiritual growth especially being able to see how things we dwell on colour our whole thought world. It's hardly surprising that I dream so much about cricket! I've even played for England in my dreams! When I was ill my dreams were often traumatic - frequently I seemed to be struggling to get to take a Service in Church and everything was frustrating me from getting there! At other times they were full of fear and terror, especially because I felt I was being attacked.

This whole process of spiritual growth was much impeded when my mind was flooded with the unwanted intrusive thoughts. It began to pick up steam once I had begun to gain some mastery over these thanks largely to the medication which relieved the anxiety.

As far as forgiveness was concerned I recalled a sermon that I had heard a Lay Reader give a few years previously. He had urged the importance of praying for people we dislike as well as those we like, and indeed to pray for those who have wronged us in anyway.

I brought back into my conscious mind all those incidents where this applied. I sought forgiveness from God both for them and for myself if I had in any way contributed to the problem. Also I sought forgiveness for any hurt I had caused to anyone. This again I found to be therapeutic.

Many patients and parishioners that I meet have this crippling burden on their backs. Either they cannot accept God's forgiveness for themselves, or are unable to extend forgiveness to those who have wronged or hurt them. This of course is a big factor in much physical as well as mental illness. It was very true of several on the ward where I was a patient - many of them were beset with faulty relationships that needed the ingredient of forgiveness.

Here is a big area of life where the spiritual dimension is so relevant to the needs of people - so much a part of health and wholeness. I recalled comments in Douglas Webster's book 'In Debt to Christ'[32] where he shows that it is usually those who have suffered severely at the hands of others who are the most forgiving.

A remarkable fairly recent example would be that of Gordon Wilson. His nursing daughter Marie was tragically killed by the terrorist bomb outrage one Remembrance Sunday at Enniskillen. As he puts in his book 'Marie', "Human beings may be, can be, and indeed ought to be, able to forgive on human terms, but ultimately it is for God to forgive, and on his terms .... I'm not going to add to the hatreds by talking about bitterness or revenge. I'll go on praying for all of them and leave the rest to God. That's the only way I can handle it and still live with myself."[33]

Again this shows the strength of the Cross of Jesus, God being able to do with us and through us what we could never do for ourselves. Gordon Wilson's understanding of forgiveness has helped reconciliation in his own community. He has been a powerful example to many. He has received sackfuls of letters.

It has been pointed out that the Cross is made up of two beams, the vertical and the cross beam, which Jesus carried. The vertical beam can be said to represent the forgiveness of God reaching down to us, the cross beam representing the forgiveness that we need to extend to each other. *Together* they make up the Cross.

I always remember visiting Coventry Cathedral and in the ruins of the old Cathedral, bombed during World War II, at the east end, seeing the two scarred timbers made into a Cross. Behind on the wall are the words 'Father forgive' - very eloquent in their testimony.

My time in hospital gave me opportunity to ponder the reality of God's forgiveness and what a hard but fulfilling road it can be. I began to realise more also the cost to God and to see it all more in terms of the healing of relationships rather than remission of punishment.

Speaking of Christ's agony and the cost of our sin to the heart of God, William Temple writes, "We cannot go on wounding One who accepts our wounds like that: we are filled with fear, not the old craven fear of punishment, but the fear of wounding the tenderest of all hearts."[34]

During my illness I came to a new appreciation of the Psalms, especially of Psalm 139 with its theme that as well as our search for God, life is above all about God's search for us, and that He is with us in the darkness as well as in the light.

"Lord, you have searched me and you know me.
You know when I sit and when I rise;
You perceive my thoughts from afar.
Where can I go from your Spirit?
Where can I flee from your presence?
If I go up to the heavens, you are there;
If I make my bed in the depths you are there.
If I say, 'surely the darkness will hide me
and light become night around me,'
Even the darkness will not be dark to you;
the night will shine like the day
for darkness is as light to you".[35]

The climax of all this is the Cross where we uniquely find God or rather where He uniquely finds us - we find ourselves loved and accepted by Him.

Another avenue of spiritual growth came through the fact that as a patient I was on the receiving end of help and that I needed to learn to accept it in the right spirit. It's not just pride that hold us back from this. It's the fact that so many of us are so used to giving care by nature of our work or role in life that it can seem strange or even threatening to admit our own needs, and to receive graciously. I suppose that's why it's said that some nurses make poor patients.

In Christian terms generally we are taught so often the need to give. However, we need to recall also the Gospel narratives where Jesus received what was offered to Him, for example, his anointing at Bethany. He received that offering as a gift of love. We in fact rob people of the opportunity to show love if we won't receive. As has been pointed out a constant urge to be needed can be a subtle form of taking.

For a long time prayer itself was very difficult as I just could not concentrate. I couldn't even concentrate to read the cricket scores in the papers so I knew I had problems! The intrusive bad thoughts would overwhelm me in the Hospital Chapel also when I tried to worship.

It was later when I got more control over my thoughts that I came to be more disciplined about my prayer life than ever before. This was particularly about prayer first thing in the morning as well as at night.

In particular I came to appreciate more the importance of putting the day into God's hands for His protecting, guiding power, not just for myself but also those for whom I was praying. This I linked with the passage in Ephesians chapter 6 about the whole armour of God - consciously putting on the various pieces of spiritual equipment to tackle the various strains and stresses of life. This is a discipline I sustain each morning. I remind myself that I've done so if fears intrude into my mind. It is one way of quelling them.

"Stand firm then, with the belt of truth around your waist, with the breastplate of righteousness in place, and with your feet fitted with the readiness that comes from the gospel of peace. In addition to all this take up the shield of faith, with which you can extinguish all the flaming arrows of the evil one. Take the helmet of salvation and the sword of the Spirit, which is the Word of God. And pray in the Spirit on all occasions with all kinds of prayers and requests."[36]

I also began to use as a daily early morning prayer the following great hymn:-

"God be in my head and in my understanding;
God be in my eyes and in my looking;
God be in my mouth and in my speaking;
God be in my heart and in my thinking;
God be at my end and at my departing."[37]

So I learned to start each day with positive prayerful thinking.

At times as I witnessed the strong bond that some sufferers had with God, I was reminded of Dora Greenwell's words on looking to Christ crucified, "I wasn't met with cold platitudes but from the eyes of Him who was indeed acquainted with grief with a look of solemn recognition that might pass between friends who have shared together some secret sorrow, and are by it united in a bond that cannot be broken."[38]

Many found it a great strength to realise that God was sharing in their suffering, fortifying them, not laying the suffering on them. Some would be bitter in their sufferings, some would gain an extra dimension to life. This spiritual dimension is a sharing already in Christ's Easter victory, an approach to life and a quality of life that nothing can destroy.

The living God meets us in our strengths as well as in our weaknesses. He meets us in the talents and gifts He entrusts to us, for those with eyes to see this. Again and again we witness the triumph of the human spirit.

Since the sixth form at school I have had great admiration for the writings of the eminent historian Sir Herbert Butterfield. In the course of an essay on the prospect for Christianity he writes that the unique feature of the life of the Churches is their insistence that the spiritual dimension is the key to life as a whole. It is centred in communion with the living Christ and the actual practice of the spiritual life.

In another passage he has this to say, ... "in all ages there have been forms of worldliness sufficient to daunt anybody attached to the life of the Spirit: in all ages the redeeming feature of the story has lain precisely where it lies at the present day - namely, in the fact that amid superstition, indifference, mere conventionality, and worldliness, there always were genuine Christians attached to the spiritual life, genuine Christians doing what they were always told they would have to do, bearing their cross, not knowing whether their work would have results, but just leaving the consequences to Providence."[39]

Easter vindicates all the truths for which Christ died and lives - love, forgiveness, reconciliation, justice, caring, sharing, health and wholeness etc. We can be assured in following these truths we're on to the real thing - to the real secret of what life is all about, both here and hereafter. Here is the basis for all our spiritual and moral values. Here is the power to lift inner burdens from minds and hearts. There is a very moving passage in John Bunyan's 'Pilgrim's Progress' when Christian finds the burden of his inner conflicts lifted from his back as he faces the Cross and Resurrection of Jesus. "Then was Christian glad and lithesome, and said, with a merry heart, 'He hath given me rest by His sorrow and life by His death'."

One of my heroes, that great visionary Vaughan Williams has clothed this in wonderful music in his Fifth Symphony, "describing the nature of true peace in the hearts of those who like Christian in 'Pilgrim's Progress' have faced their conflicts and come through them."

As I spent hours on hospital wards talking and praying with a cross section of humanity, again and again I faced with them the unfairness of much in life. To be able to help people to see that God in Christ shares in all this, and that ultimately things do get sorted out, brought much reassurance to many.

It is of course supremely through the Cross that God shares in the injustices of life. In Luke's account of the death of Jesus, the Centurion says, "Beyond all doubt this man was innocent."[40] Jesus certainly experienced injustice in witnessing to the truth and so He shares with all who suffer unjustly. Easter proves the rightness of all for which He lived and died.. Thus in Christ no unjust suffering is in vain.

It was humbling and heartening to see many people coming to spiritual victory over their tribulation and traumas. It provided evidence for the truth of Butterfield's view that ...... "the long term results of history would seem to vindicate the power of the spiritual more than anything else....."

Here were people in actual experience working out the truth of all this. Experience is the surest of testing grounds. I love the story of the conversation between Ernest Bevin and King George VI when Bevin was appointed Foreign Secretary after the 1945 Election. The King had a great regard for Bevin who had held high office in the War-time Coalition Government. He was amazed that someone from such humble origins had such knowledge of the world and enquired of Bevin how this know-how had come. Bevin replied, "I plucked it from the hedgerows of experience."[41]

The proof of the Christian faith comes through experience. From the first it has been concerned with realities. The questions in effect that people ask of it are "Is it true? Does it work?" These are the questions we need to address.

CHAPTER 7
MEDICATION HELP

In the 1950's a major break-through in the treatment of people with mental illness came with the discovering of the chemical factor in much of it, and the production of medication to deal with this. As a result, for example, in the treatment of schizophrenia, one third of patients can now be cured, and another third have their condition controlled so as to live a normal life. Only in a third of cases does it remain chronic.

Depression very much lends itself to treatment by medication and anti-depressants are not addictive. An anti-depressant called parstelin helped greatly to lift the depression of my illness. The bad intrusive thoughts were then reduced both in their intensity and frequency, and anxiety levels lowered. This meant that I was able to get much more control over them, and be in a position to dismiss them more quickly from my mind. The positive thoughts were reinforced and I could concentrate more.

I began to regain my confidence and could converse much more freely. The big reduction in the obsessive thoughts also was matched by a big reduction in the checkings and other rituals. It was as if I was being released from my chains. It became easier to bring into effect the behavioural techniques of dealing with the obsessive thoughts, now that a lot of the anxiety had gone.

There was improvement in my physical and spiritual health as well as my mental health. I was able to participate more in prayer and worship. I don't exaggerate when I say it was like a resurrection. I was motivated to press on in earnest with the uphill climb to recovery. I even had hopes that I might be able to play cricket again!

It brought home to me in a new way the truth that the resurrection that God in Christ makes possible in us is not only with regard to the future life, but also with life now - new hope, new life breaking through even the most traumatic situations. Significantly I wanted to reach out to others with something of the new depth of love that God had given me.

As Harry Williams puts it in his book 'True Resurrection', "When here and now we have known ourselves raised from the dead, we have in that experience apprehended ourselves as being somehow created by a power which is beyond us."[42] Earlier in the book he had written, "When we begin to recognise the power of resurrection present in the ordinary gritty routine of our daily lives, then we shall see for ourselves that all that separates and injures and destroys is being overcome by what unites and heals and creates."[43]

This is part of the proof that Christ lives, the truth of Easter, namely how He transforms human life in the here and now. He fills us with love for Him and love for people - the evidence of transformed lives.

I also began to get a new insight into mental illness. I realised the importance of the chemical factor. I believe many of the general public to be ignorant about this. They tend to think the medication just consists of tranquilizers and the like. They don't appreciate the bio-chemical factor in much of the illness. If they did they would be more sympathetic and less prone to making stupid remarks such as "pull yourself together" which just increases the patient's sense of distress. Stress or other factors, such as a shock or trauma, can produce a fluctuation in the chemistry of the mind and this can affect people's thoughts and moods. A classic example of the influence of the chemical factor can be seen in post-natal depression. It is very heartening to see many young mothers with that problem well on their way to recovery after a few weeks of medical treatment nowadays.

Obviously there was a chemical factor in my own illness and it was the parstelin medication that met that need and gave me greater control over my thoughts. It shows the way that God works through medication as well as prayer. Many obsessional patients are helped by the anti-depressants, clomipramine or fluvoxamine. A book published in 1990 entitled 'Obsessive Compulsive Disorder' says "there is reason to believe that the combination of a 5-HT re-uptake inhibitor and behaviour therapy is presently the most effective treatment of OCD"[44] (Obsessive Compulsive Disorder). Clomipramine and fluvoxamine are 5-HT re-uptake inhibitors.

People with high and low states of mood are helped to get on to an even keel by a medication like lithium carbonate. Incidentally, it is interesting to see how the Gospels tell of the use of medication by Jesus Himself in His work of health and wholeness in those days. The spittle of a holy person was believed to have therapeutic properties. He uses that as He touches the tongue of the deaf man (Mark chapter 7). In healing the blind man, as recorded in St. John chapter 9, He used His saliva and some mud to make a paste and put it on the patient's eyes.

The Book of Ecclesiasticus, chapter 38, has a splendid passage on the value of medication, "The Lord has created medicine from the earth and a sensible man will not disparage them. The Lord has imparted knowledge to men, that by use of his marvels he may win praise; by using them the doctor relieves pain and from them the pharmacist makes up his mixture."[45]

The medication helped me to find release too from the pressure and tension feelings in my head. I began to feel much more positive about life in general. The medication can break the stranglehold of the intrusive thoughts and fears and give us some measure of control. We are then able to assist more in our own recovery, especially with the help of the behavioural techniques taught by the psychologist. This is in line with the medical view expressed by Beech and Vaughan, "the combined use of drugs and behaviour therapy warrant close attention, as it seems likely that eventually it may be demonstrated that neither treatment is entirely effective on its own."[46] I have certainly been helped by that combination, together with the spiritual help.

So many people need that initial medical help. Would that more would seek it earlier and get that lift up on to the ladder leading out of the pit! You can't sort it out on your own.

CHAPTER 8
PSYCHOLOGICAL HELP - BEHAVIOUR THERAPY

A psychologist pointed out to me that by certain strategies people can chip away at and slowly weaken obsessive thoughts. This requires a lot of hard effort, wise advice and a supportive atmosphere. When a bad or distressing thought comes we must see it for what it is and dismiss it as quickly as possible from our mind. We must not begin to brood on it or analyse it. Part of the dismissive strategy is to say "mental rubbish" when such thoughts come and not to give them credence. We can put an elastic band round our wrist and twang it to distract us away from the thought. That and other thought-stopping techniques are encouraged: something that will distract our attention away from the bad thought; perhaps a quick glance round the room to fasten on an object that will break the thought pattern, or to switch on the radio. The more we can avoid giving an immediate response to the thoughts the more they will gradually recede. We will never in fact say or write such thoughts - people with the problem never do. We need to remember that we are flawed human beings, it is part of the human condition when these perfectionist traits try and take over.

The compulsive urge to check is strong at first causing great anxiety, but as we employ the dismissive strategies they gradually get less, both in intensity and frequency. It is reasonable to read through a letter once and to check once that a door is locked or a switch in the proper position, but that must be the limit. All urges to check more than once must be resisted or they intensify the problem.

In dismissing the thoughts we need to switch quickly to a positive or happy thought. It is a help to soak the mind in one or two positive thoughts. Then we can more quickly switch to these and thus prevent the development of ruminations. Also if we are thinking of nothing in particular these positive thoughts will tend to be the first that spin off the top of our head - so we are less vulnerable. This is true when for example the telephone or the door-bell ring. The pressure of these, instead of being an opening for the bad thoughts, will be met by these positive thoughts that we have deliberately cultivated.

It certainly requires a lot of disciplined mental effort over a long period to reach that point. However it is really worth it for the help it gives in gradually mastering the problem.

Conversation is made easier when we learn how to deal with bad thoughts about people. Instead of introducing a balancing statement into conversation, just inwardly say to yourself a good thought about that person.

Often the mind can be like a battle-field between positive thoughts and intrusive negative thoughts, and we can become mentally exhausted, but we have got to sustain the fight if we are going to win through. The times I have said "mental rubbish!"

In no way are we going insane nor is our brain disintegrating. The problem is in our thought patterns. These are tied up with the chemistry of our mind. So the chemicals in the anti-depressant are addressed to rectifying this by strengthening the positive signals. Certainly these obsessive thoughts are not God's will for us but the tyrant of fear caused by them takes a lot of dislodging. Our mind is so pre-occupied. Just the routine things of everyday life are a colossal ordeal.

If we have phobias about electrical appliances or glass or dirt we need to be helped with a therapy which exposes us to these elements so that we can handle these things and gradually master our panic about them. As we persevere then in time the anxiety begins to recede.

As we recover a sense of humour it helps this process. I recall the famous conductor, Sir Malcolm Sargent, saying on the 'Brain's Trust' on B.B.C. Radio that a sense of humour is basically putting a relative value on yourself. He rated this as one of the basic qualities needed for life along with loving-kindness, the art of loving our fellow human-beings as ourselves, and faith, ordinary Christian faith. "Given faith, life can remain an exciting adventure and even death can lose its sting."[47]

Dynamic therapy tackles the root of the psychological problem. Behaviour therapy is geared towards removing the presenting symptoms.

It is a great help when someone with insight listens to our story. By opening themselves to our mental stress and anguish they can be a real healing influence as they assure us of our unique value. So they counter our low self-esteem, and give us a feeling of worth. This is a powerful way of our being affirmed in the love of God. Many pastorally minded Christians could help with this.

CHAPTER 9
THE WOUNDED HELPER

All this experience of mental illness has helped me to understand more the role of Jesus as wounded helper. His mental pain was as real as his physical suffering. That is clear from the Gospel accounts of the agony in the Garden of Gethsemane as well as on the Cross. So He shares with us in the mental suffering as well as in our physical suffering in a very personal way.

It has strengthened my belief that Christianity should above all be concerned with personal values, the source and inspiration for those values being in the loving personality of God. All the great advances achieved by science and technology must not blind us to the priority of people and their search for meaning - to know that they are loved and wanted and that they have an eternal destiny which nothing can destroy. That assurance comes through personal encounter with Jesus - our wounded Helper. We can be led through the trauma of mental illness to an even deeper personal trust in Jesus and His love for us.

We do well to ponder the words of Mother Teresa, "People may look different, or be dressed differently, or have a different education or position, but they are all the same. They are all people to be loved. They are all hungry for love."

Many people in suffering are struggling to come to grips with life's meaning, some of them for the first time in a really deep way. British people are reluctant to go public about their spiritual feelings, seeing them as essentially a private issue, but many in suffering are ready to open up and talk about the things that really matter. In particular I have experienced the way in which many value prayer. Indeed some hold out their hand for it to be clasped as I pray quietly with them. Some I notice have tears in their eyes after such prayer. I feel very much the presence and power of God, and recall the poet Tennyson's words, "More things are wrought by prayer than this world dreams of."

Some mentally ill people have bizarre religious beliefs, but most seek an authentic relationship with God. Personal contacts enable you to correct mistaken ideas that people have about God, helping them to see that God is love.

There is so much fear to be overcome and if people's view of God is a harsh censorious one, their fears are reinforced rather than released. It seems to come as a surprise to many that God's essential nature is love. He shares in our wounds and deepens our capacity for self-giving love. That is above all how He is our wounded Helper.

I find much inspiration in the 'Wounded Healer' passages in Isaiah 53 and 1 Peter. Jesus tackles suffering on the Cross without giving us an explanation of it, but giving us the faith and courage to cope. He shows us how suffering can be accepted and transformed by sympathy, love and sacrifice. It can produce a real sense of sharing, a concern for others and a quality of fellowship that nothing else can. Speaking of the power of self-giving love, Arnold Toynbee, one of the great historians of this century, writes that "though it may appear to be swimming against the tide, the secret currents of the universe flow in that direction."

To share in this self-giving love is to experience a real inner healing even though the afflictions may remain. Our final healing awaits us in heaven. Our theme of Jesus as the wounded Helper and its implications for our following of Him are well expressed in Amy Carmichael's poem, 'No Scar?'

> "Hast thou no scar?
> No hidden scar on foot, or side, or hand?
> I hear thee sung as mighty in the land,
> I hear them hail thy bright ascendant star,
> Hast thou no scar?
>
> Hast thou no wound?
> Yet I was wounded by the archers, spent,
> Leaned me against a tree to die; and rent
> By ravening beasts that compassed me, I swooned:
> Hast thou no wound?
>
> No wound? No scar?
> Yet, as the Master shall the servant be,
> And pierced are the feet that follow Me:
> But thine are whole: can he have followed far
> Who has no wound nor scar?"[48]

It was a wise pastor who said, "In Love's service only the wounded soldiers can serve."

The same theme is taken up by Edward Stillito in his poem "Jesus of the Scars", and its memorable phrase, "To our wounds only God's wounds can speak."

I have learnt more about the value of the ministry of touch, prayerfully holding someone's hand, or through the laying-on of hands. It is significant to see how much Jesus used the ministry of touch in his ministry recorded in the Gospels. Much of God's care, compassion and strength can come to us that way when words seem so inadequate. I find that it is a ministry much appreciated by many with mental illness too.

There is a spiritual dimension to much mental illness and many patients do seek Christian ministry - for example those worried by a sense of guilt or unworthiness, or low self-esteem, or those ill through bereavement. We can see so much of God in their vulnerability and often we can learn from them.

It has been particularly rewarding to talk with patients suffering from obsessional states and phobias. They have found it a great sense of relief just to talk with someone who has been through a similar experience, to share insights and to discuss together ways of tackling it.

A very conscientious shop assistant who was in hospital for several months was obsessional about dust and dirt, and its power of contamination. She had a deep sense of unworthiness also and was much in need of seeing Christ as the 'wounded Helper' and His love for her. She has gradually battled through to better health, and deeper faith in God.

God is with us when the negative thoughts and fears assail us just as much as He is when we feel on top of the world - that is part of the meaning of the Cross - we can never drift beyond His love and care. He is working through the medical and spiritual channels to bring us that realisation. So we can take fresh courage. Many with fears, anxieties and other inner conflicts feel able to relate to us and share their burdens with us before God in confidence. This is yet another way in which the trauma of illness can be turned into a positive. It is humbling and inspiring to see this redemptive power of God at work in people.

It reminds me of a young student patient I have met who suffered similar difficulties to myself, and who came through and indeed came closer to God through it all. He also came into an even better relationship with his parents and his sister. He said to me, "I feel a better person."

I value very much William Cowper's hymns. He had a long struggle with mental illness which gives greater significance to his writing, for example, 'O for a closer walk with God'. You feel the poignancy of the words:-

> "O for a closer walk with God,
> A calm and heavenly frame;
> A light to shine upon the road
> That leads me to the Lamb.
>
> What peaceful hours I once enjoyed,
> How sweet their memory still!
> But they have left an aching void
> The world can never fill."

In his hymn 'God moves in a mysterious way' there comes the verse:

> "Ye fearful saints fresh courage take
> The clouds you so much dread
> Are big with mercy, and shall break
> In blessings on your head."[49]

Yes, dread has turned into blessings as so much insight has come my way through my illness, and through the assistance I have received. It has helped me to become a humbler, less judgmental, more compassionate, prayerful, and understanding person. I have come to appreciate even more the thinking behind the great saying of C.S. Lewis, "I believe in Christianity as I believe the sun has risen, not only because I see it, but because by it I see everything else."[50]

The first Epistle of St. John makes it clear that love is the greatest antidote to fear. Certainly in my illness I was surrounded by a great deal of love, much of that channelled to me medically and spiritually by my carers, by fellow patients, and by my loved ones and other praying people. One of the very positive things to emerge through all the trauma can be the way in which God increases our capacity to love - to give and receive and share love.

There is in human experience again and again this mysterious union of love and suffering. It is well described in the story of C.S. Lewis and his wife, Joy, in the book 'Shadowlands'. C.S. Lewis said of Joy, "Her courage is wonderful as she gives me more support than I can give her."[51] The suffering that loves and the love that suffers. This union is interpreted and inspired by the Cross of Jesus. There on the Cross is the meeting between human suffering and Divine Love. As someone has pointed out it is no accident that the Cross, the symbol of united love and suffering, is the badge of the world's greatest relief organisation, the Red Cross. It is the badge of the wounded Helper.

I am absolutely sure God doesn't send illness to teach us these lessons, but I'm sure He does help us to respond positively to such experiences and to be of help to those struggling with similar darkness. That's why we can 'fresh courage take'.

NOTES

1. Essentials of Postgraduate Psychiatry, 2nd Edition, Edited by Hill, Murray & Thooley, p.211. Grune & Stretton.
2. St. Mark 15 v 34. New International Version, Hodder & Stoughton.
3. 'The Atonement', p.174, F.R. Barry, Hodder & Stoughton.
4. Henderson & Gillespies's Textbook of Psychiatry, 10th Edition p.66, Oxford University Press.
5. 'Healing the Hurt Mind', p.20-21, Dr. David Enoch, Hodder & Stoughton.
6. Henderson & Gillespie's Textbook of Psychiatry, 10th Edition p.162, Oxford University Press.
7. 'The Observer' newspaper magazine 18.3.90 Dr. Judith Rapoport article on 'Obsessive Compulsive Disorder, an extract from 'The boy who coundn't stop washing', Collins.
8. 'Living by Faith', p.345, Stuart Blanch, Darton, Longman & Todd. Stuart Blanch was Archbishop of York 1975-83.
9. Psalm 55 v. 5-6, N.I.V.
10. Psalm 57 v. 6 Ibid.
11. Psalm 13 v. 2 Ibid.
12. Mapperley Hospital, Nottingham - a hospital with a great history that has done much to pioneer modern mental health care, especially during the leadership of Dr Duncan Macmillan during the years 1941-66. By October 1952 all wards in the hospital were unlocked making Mapperley the first fully open mental hospital in England.
13. 'Sharing the Darkness', p.157, Sheila Cassidy, Darton, Longman & Todd.
14. F.R. Barry in Southwell Diocesan Newsletter, February 1955.
15. 'Period of my Life', p.195, F.R. Barry, Hodder & Stoughton.
16. 'Good Friday People', p.12, Sheila Cassidy, Darton, Longman & Todd.
17. 'To recover Confidence', p.18-19, F.R.Barry, S.C.M.
18. Romans 8 v. 38-39, N.I.V.
19. 'To be a Pilgrim', Basil Hume, St. Paul Publications.
20. 'Journey to Wholeness', p.82, Bishop Morris Maddocks, S.P.C.K.
21. Sir John Stallworthy in Sermon from St. Aldates ed. Canon Keith de Berry p.106, Hodder & Stoughton.
22. 'We Believe in Healing', Dr. Ruth Fowke, edited by Dr. Ann England, Highland Books.
23. 'What is Spiritual Healing?', p.5, Canon Douglas Webster, Highway Press.
24. 'I Believe in the Holy Spirit', p.175, Canon Michael Green, Hodder & Stoughton.
25. 'Through the Year with J.B. Phillips', p.104, J.B. Phillips, Hodder & Stoughton.
26. St. John 1 v.5, Revised Standard Version.
27. 'The Heart of Healing', p. 125, Canon George Bennett, Arthur James.

[28]. Institute of Religion & Medicine Journal, Sir James Watt article p.20-29, December 1991.
[29]. 'The Art of the Possible', p.177, R.A. Butler, Hamish Hamilton.
[30]. 'The Observer' Newspaper Magazine 18.3.96, Dr. Peter Dally.
[31]. Philippians 4 v. 8 N.I.V.
[32]. 'In Debt to Christ', p.36-37, Douglas Webster, Highway Press.
[33]. 'Marie', p.92, Gordon Wilson, Marshall & Pickering.
[34]. 'The Faith & Modern Thought', p.135, William Temple.
[35]. Psalm 139 vs. 1,2,7,8,11,12 N.I.V.
[36]. Ephesians 6 v. 14-18 N.I.V.
[37]. Pynson's Horae 1514.
[38]. Article by Dora Greenwell.
[39]. 'Writings on Christianity & History', p.250, Sir Herbert Butterfield, Oxford University Press.
[40]. Luke 23 v. 47, New English Bible.
[41]. 'The Private Office', p.37 Nicholas Henderson, Weidenfeld & Nicolson.
[42]. 'The Resurrection', p.176, Harry Williams, Mitchell Beazley.
[43]. Ibid. p.12-13.
[44]. 'Obsessive Compulsive Disorder', Ed. Montgomery, Goodman Goeting. Duphar Medical Relations.
[45]. Ecclesiasticus 38 v. 4,6,7 New English Bible.
[46]. 'Behavioural Treatment of Obsessional States', p.153 Beech & Vaughan, John Wiley & Sons.
[47]. 'Malcolm Sargent', p.330, Charles Reid, Hodder & Stoughton.
[48]. 'Towards Jerusalem', p.85, Amy Carmichael.
[49]. William Cowper (1731-1800) was a lay assistant to the Rev. John Newton, Vicar of Olney in Buckinghamshire. Together they produced the Olney Hymn Book including many hymns that are now basic to the repertoire. The exact nature of his mental illness is not known.
[50]. 'They asked for a Paper', p165, C.S. Lewis, Bles.
[51]. 'Shadowlands', p.133, Brian Sibley, Hodder & Stoughton.

MOORLEY'S

...are growing Publishers, adding several new titles to our list each year. We also undertake private publications and commissioned works.

Our range of publications includes: **Books of Verse**
　　　　　　Devotional Poetry
　　　　　　Recitations
　　　　　　Drama
　　　　　　Bible Plays
　　　　　　Sketches
　　　　　　Nativity Plays
　　　　　　Passiontide Plays
　　　　　　Easter Plays
　　　　　　Demonstrations
　　　　　　Resource Books
　　　　　　Assembly Material
　　　　　　Songs & Musicals
　　　　　　Children's Addresses
　　　　　　Prayers & Graces
　　　　　　Daily Readings
　　　　　　Books for Speakers
　　　　　　Activity Books
　　　　　　Quizzes
　　　　　　Puzzles
　　　　　　Painting Books
　　　　　　Daily Readings
　　　　　　Church Stationery
　　　　　　Notice Books
　　　　　　Cradle Rolls
　　　　　　Hymn Board Numbers

Please send a S.A.E. (approx 9" x 6") for the current catalogue or consult your local Christian Bookshop who should stock or be able to order our titles.